MILLERS POINT SONGBOOK

Music and lyrics by Joanna Weinberg

JAMES HART
NARRATOR

ROB JOHNSON
CAPTAIN GRIMES, ERNEST ANTHONY, SYDNEY HARBOUR TRUST OFFICIAL

ELIANE MOREL
SINGER: SUNBED, LEADER WCTU, GEORGINA LONG, ESTATE AGENT, MIDWIFE

BILLIE PALIN
MARY UNDERWOOD, OUTRAGED WHARFIE, MIDWIFE, WASHERWOMAN, RAT

ANNEROSE DE JONG
MAYBANKE ANDERSON, NITA McCRAE, WASHERWOMAN, SHEEP

MUSICAL DIRECTOR
MICHELLE GOLDMAN
PIANO, KEYS

PAUL MISKIN
BANJO, GUITAR, BASS

JEREMY COOK
PERCUSSION, DRUMS

DIRECTOR
JOANNA WEINBERG

SOUND
JASON DE WILDE

LIGHTING
LARRY KELLY

SETS & COSTUMES
GAV BARBEY

ASST. COSTUME DESIGNERS / COSTUME MAKERS
VALI McDONALD &
DRUSILLA SELENE

CORMAC CHAMPION
JACK MUNDEY

FRANCISCA VAN WEL
MEL TAIT

CHRIS RUSSELL
LIEUTENANT DAWES

JOANNA WEINBERG
ANNE KIRKMAN

CHRIS MURPHY
DRUNK NURSEY

CRAIG KEELER-MILNE &
HARLEY NASH
HEAVIES

CHOIR ROCKS
MARGARET BISHOP
CORMAC CHAMPION
ANNEROSE DE JONG
KATHRYN DRUMMOND
JAMES HART
SUE HUNT
CRAIG KEELER-MILNE
JENNIFER KEELER-MILNE
DOT KOLENTSIS
MICHELLE McDONALD
CHRIS MURPHY
HARLEY NASH
MAJA SKRLS-TUFEGDZIC
CHRIS RUSSELL
MICHAEL RUSSELL
FRANCISCA VAN WEL
GRAHAM WILSON

ADDITIONAL MUSIC & LYRICS
SUE HUNT

PUBLICITY
GEOFF SIRMAI

FROM AN ONGOING IDEA BY
ANNE WARR

PRODUCERS
JOANNA WEINBERG
ANNE WARR
MARGARET BISHOP
JOHN DUNN

PROGRAM EDITOR & DESIGNER
JOHN DUNN

ACKNOWLEDGEMENTS

Thank you to our supporters

Kerr Neilson

Margaret Bishop & John Dunn

Melanie Tait & Jules Comin

Robert Hannan & Peter Crawshaw

David Barry & Neil Glaser

Jennie Gao & Greg Ainsworth

Mandy Nikpour & Marc Pellegrini

1922 HARBOUR VIEW HOTEL

CITY OF SYDNEY

CHURCH HILL The Garrison ANGLICAN

The Australiana Society
Research, Collecting, Preservation

NSW GOVERNMENT

CARTER WILLIAMSON

BRIDGECLIMB SYDNEY

VIVID SYDNEY LIGHT, MUSIC & IDEAS

McGrath

The Millers Point Songbook first performed during Vivid at The Garrison Church on 24, 25, 26, 27 and 28 May 2024

ISBN 978-1-7635761-0-0

MILLERS POINT SONGBOOK

BILLIARDS
YOUNG PRINCESS INN
LONDON PORTER

PROLOGUE

The Argyle Cut opened in 1859. Stone quarried during its construction was used in building the Garrison Church, which now sits beneath the cliff-face and faces a small park the locals call the Village Green.

On the northern side of the Village Green are the houses of Argyle Place, mostly built from the 1820s and 1840s, and once home to Captain Grimes, Mary Underwood, John Fair-fax and James Merriman, amongst others.

Argyle Place is at the heart of Millers Point. In 2021, local resident, Anne Warr was awarded a Heritage NSW Community Grant for an Argyle Place Interpretation Plan which included seed funding for a theatrical performance. Joanna Weinberg was invited to write music and lyrics for a theatrical performance which would include the choir. Joanna used existing historic material and researched more to write lyrics about people and pivotal moments in the development of Millers Point.

The *Millers Point Songbook* celebrates, in text and music, the characters of Millers Point. Residents from Colonial times to the present are portrayed, including Captain Grimes and Mary Underwood; Lieutenant Dawes and Patyegarang; Nita McCrae and Jack Mundey; and Myra and the residents of Sirius. The famous, the infamous, the colourful and the ordinary residents of Millers Point are brought to life in the *Millers Point Songbook*.

The five performances of the *Millers Point Songbook* at the Garrison Church are the cumination of a creative snowball that has become a true community production.

The production is supported by a City of Sydney Festivals and Events grant that was awarded to Anne Warr in 2023, as well as significant donations from local residents, generous support from the Garrison Church and local businesses, volunteers working behind the scenes, and the members of Choir Rocks who appreciate this opportunity to perform alongside outstanding professional singers and musicians. Our thanks go to all who contributed to this production, including the audiences who are supporting the *Millers Point Songbook* by being here!

IMAGES

front cover and pages 14–15
Charles Walton, *Rocks laneway (Downshire Street, Dawes Point)*, c.1935, silver gelatin photoprint, State Library of New South Wales

pages 4–5
Joseph Fowles, *Millers Point (from Flagstaff Hill looking down Fort Street)*, c.1845, watercolour, State Library of New South Wales

pages 12
Geoff Sirmai, *Joanna Weinberg and Choir Rocks*

pages 30
Richard Briggs, *Save Our Souls*, pen on paper

inside back cover
Freeman brothers, *Panorama from Observatory Hill*, c.1858, published 1867, State Library of New South Wales

back cover
Joseph Fowles, *Millers Point (from Flagstaff Hill looking over Argyle and Kent Streets)*, c.1845, watercolour, State Library of New South Wales

JAMES HART

James Hart over many years has performed across many areas of the entertainment arena. He started out singing in rock and soul bands, then moved into acting, performing in musical theatre, drama and comedy.
James has been a professional tour guide undertaking tours around the Rocks area for twelve years during both the day and evening.
James has been employed by Sydney University to conduct tours through the Sydney Conservatorium of Music for the general public and school groups.
James has worked for a company specialising in exclusive tours guiding small groups through the Blue Mountains and around Sydney Harbour in a 1960s EK Holden Sedan.
James is passionate about sharing his knowledge of Sydney's history, especially its people, and bringing their fascinating stories alive.

ROB JOHNSON

Rob Johnson is an actor and writer based in the Southern Highlands of New South Wales. Acting credits include *The Boomkak Panto*, *Calamity Jane* [Belvoir]; *The Torrents* [Sydney Theatre Company]; *Spamalot*, *Gypsy* [One Eyed Man]; *The Detective's Handbook*, *Musical Bang Bang* [Hayes Theatre Co]; *Of Thee I Sing* [Sydney Philharmonia Choirs]; *Babies Proms: The Four Seasons* [CDP/ Sydney Opera House]; *Man of La Mancha*, *Carrie*, *Sondheim on Sondheim*, *Triassic Parq*, *Good Omens* [Squabbalogic]; *Rosehaven* [ABC]; *Random & Whacky* [Network 10]; and *Sheilas* [Screen Australia]. For his performance as Francis Fryer in *Calamity Jane*, Rob was nominated for the Green Room Award, Sydney Theatre Award, and Glug Award for Best Supporting Actor in a Musical. He is a two-time NSW Theatresports Champion, and was a national finalist for the 2020 Second City/CBS Comedy Scholarship.
Rob's fiction, non-fiction and poetry have been published widely; for the stage, he has written *The Recidivists* [Red Line Productions]
Rob will next be seen in Musical *Bang Bang* at the Adelaide Cabaret Festival in June.

ELIANE MOREL

Eliane Morel is a Sydney-based writer/actor/singer, graduate of the NIDA writers' program and the Canberra School of Music, currently a principal Mezzo with Sydney's favourite boutique opera company, Opera Bites [Rosina *Barber of Seville*, Carmen *Carmen*, Prince Orlofsky *Die Fledermaus*, Mrs Page *The Merry Wives of Windsor*]. Her own plays include *The Cabbage Patch Kid* [Griffin Theatre], *There was no Frog* [The Performance Space], and solo shows *An Evening with Madam Long* [The Performance Space] and *Ba Ngoai* [4A Theatre]. *Disenchanted*, her first cabaret, created with Daryl Wallis, has been performed at the Sydney, Newcastle, Dubbo, Adelaide, and Brisbane Fringes, and received awards for Best Show in Dubbo and Newcastle. Daryl and Eliane collaborated with Ghillian Sullivan to create 'Carmen the Cabaret', which debuted at the Adelaide Fringe 2023, has since played to full houses all over NSW and the ACT, was nominated for four awards at Newcastle Fringe 2024, and won the award for Artistic Merit. In 2023 Eliane played Maria in Joanna Weinberg's musical, *La Luna*, and Mrs Bailey in Joining the Dots Theatre's *It's a Wonderful Life*.

BILLIE PALIN

Originally from Dubbo, Billie Palin began her vocal training at the Macquarie Conservatorium and went on to complete a Bachelor of Music at the Australian Institute of Music. Billie's credits include *HMS Pinafore* [Ralph Rackstraw], *Godspell* [Jesus] and swing for both *Dubbo Championship Wrestling* and *Jekyll & Hyde* for The Hayes Theatre Company, *The Lovers Workshop* for Bell Shakespeare, *On a Clear Day You Can See Forever* [Muriel & Mrs Hatch] for Squabbalogic, *A Christmas Carol* for Ensemble Theatre, and the national tour of *Once* for Darlinghurst Theatre Company. Most recently she has appeared in CDP theatre producers touring production of *Ratburger* [Sheila/Tina].
Her powerhouse voice saw Billie crowned the 2019 winner of the Sydney Cabaret Competition with her cabaret 'From Dubbo to Death.'

ANNEROSE DE JONG

Annerose is an actor, director, teacher, costume, props and set designer. She is founder and artistic director at Imagination Theatre, a school dedicated to inspiring creativity, developing communication and life skills and building confidence through theatre-based activities.
As principal artist for REM Theatre 1990–2000, Annerose toured throughout Australia, Fiji and South Korea. As artistic director/performer for Self-Raising Theatre 1988–1994, she toured throughout Australia and was awarded Best Actor at the Asian Festival of Drama in Kuala Lumpur. Annerose performed her one-woman show *Dr Seuss Stories* for many years before joining the Cubby House Band as lead singer and receiving an Aria Award nomination for Best Children's Album.
With a special interest in working with people of disability, Annerose has set up drama groups and created shows to empower students to have a voice in the community, build confidence in their everyday lives and to nurture a love for theatre.
In 2023 Annerose played the cameo roles in Joanna Weinberg's new musical *La Luna*.

GAV BARBEY

Gav Barbey works and collaborates across multiple disciplines. Trained in commercial arts and awarded by NIDA a degree in theatre and film studies, majoring in production/set and costume design, he has been 24 years an exhibiting visual artist and filmmaker. He has worked within the corporate and education sectors as a facilitator in human-centred design, ideation and critical thinking, and community engagement.
Assistant Costume Designers and Costume Makers are Val McDonald and Drusilla Selene.

VAL McDONALD

DRUSILLA SELENE

MICHELLE GOLDMAN

Michelle Goldman has extensive experience as a pianist/vocalist, accompanist, repetiteur and musical director. Michelle was MD for Joanna Weinberg's *La Luna* (world premiere, March 2023) having previously played for Weinberg's *Baroness Bianka's Bloodsongs* (Camelot Lounge). For many years, Michelle regularly accompanied choirs and played for musicals at the Emanuel School, Sydney, including productions of *Oliver!*, *Fiddler on the Roof* and *Legally Blonde.* Michelle has played at numerous Shir Madness Music Festivals (Bondi Beach Pavilion) and was on keys for Alexis Fishman's *Amy: Resurrected* (Ginger's, Darlinghurst) in 2018. More recently, Michelle accompanied the Individual Voices Choir at the OLP Choral Festival as part of Sydney WorldPride 2023 (Sydney Town Hall), the WAAPA MT graduating class of 2023 Cabaret (Foundry 616) and in October 2023, she played for the comedy revue *You Don't Have To Be Jewish* (David Spicer Productions). Michelle is delighted to be playing for Weinberg's latest production, the *Millers Point Songbook*.

PAUL MISKIN

A Sydney-based musician, Paul Miskin began playing banjo and guitar at a young age. Best known as a member of Tall Tales and True, his performances have taken him across Australia and around the world. Paul's talents have earned him nominations for ARIA and AFI awards. He is thrilled to be playing in The Millers Point Songbook.

SUE HUNT

With many years' experience in school, university and community choirs, Sue Hunt works with contemporary vocal groups as a performer, teacher, conductor, composer, lyricist and arranger. The *Millers Point Songbook* marks her professional debut as a reflective musical voice of our times.

JEREMY COOK

Jeremy is a graduate of Sydney University (B Mus Jazz), a Music Board travel/study grant to New York and the road.
He has performed, recorded and waited in transit lounges with the likes of Mic Conway's National Junk Band, Captain Matchbox, Pardon Me Boys, Jeannie Lewis, Elton Jack, Blakhatz, Phil Scott, Max Gillies, Justine Clarke and most recently The Spooky Men's Chorale.
Last year's show *La Luna* from the pen of Joanna Weinberg was a fabulous experience and he is thrilled to be back working with her.
He has taught percussion for decades and, in that context, has also acted as composer, arranger and MD for numerous theatrical works, most recently *The Commitments, One Man Two Guvnors, School of Rock, Big Fish* and *The 39 Steps*.

JOANNA WEINBERG

Composer / Writer / Performer

Born in London to a family of classical musicians Joanna Weinberg spent her young adulthood in South Africa, studied drama at the University of Cape Town, and played lead roles in several plays, films and tv shows before emigrating to Australia in 1997.

Joanna is an actor, writer and composer with fourteen original one-woman shows to her name, including the critically acclaimed *Pandora's Bag, Piano Diaries, Twelve Shoes, Bianka's Bloodsongs* and *Sinksongs*, the inspiration for her internationally released feature film *Goddess*. Her award-winning musical *Lifeforce* won the Sydney Fringe Best Production award in 2013 and her soccer parent musical Every Single Saturday played in multiple Sydney theatres before touring NSW in 2011.

Recently Joanna has written, composed and directed *La Luna*, the incredible story of Gracia Nasi Mendes, a wealthy Jewish philanthropist of the Renaissance period who fled the Spanish Inquisition and saved the lives of thousands, setting up an underground network to help Jews leave Portugal.

Joanna features in the recent book *The Australian Musical* as a fresh new writing voice in musical theatre. She also directs four community choirs in Sydney. These are Joanna's professional highlights since 2011.

2011 Wrote and performed *The Piano Diaries*. Dir: Marko Mustac. [Spotify]

2012 Wrote songs and co-wrote script for *Goddess*. Dir: Mark Lamprell. [Netflix, Stan]

2013 Wrote music, book and lyrics for *Lifeforce – the Mother of All Journeys*. Dir: Lisa Freshwater.
Winner, music category Sydney Fringe.

2014 *Goddess* nomination best music: ACCI awards.

2015 Played the Duke in *Man of La Mancha* for Squabbalogic, Dir: Jay James Moody. GLUG award best musical.

2016 *Baroness Bianka's Bloodsongs*. Hayes Theatre, Butterfly Club Melbourne, Nthern Lights Theatre Canada. Dir Lisa Freshwater

2017 *Pandora's Bag* performed Hayes. Theatre and Australia-wide. [Spotify]

2018 Wrote and directed *The Secret Singer* at Eternity Playhouse. Starring Genevieve Lemon/Kate Mannix.

2018 Performed *Pandora's Bag* at Baxter Theatre Cape Town.

2019 Performed Barushka in *ONCE*. Eternity Theatre. Dir: Richard Carroll. Winner GLUG award best mainstage musical.

2019 Wrote and directed *MINKY Opens a Gallery* for Sydney Fringe.

2020 During Covid, finished composing and writing *La Luna*, two-act musical based on Beatrice de Luna AKA Gracia Nasi Mendes, the first businesswoman.

2023 Staged *La Luna, the workshop*, for five sold-out nights at Emmanuel Synagogue.

***Joanna Weinberg*, photo by Richard Weinstein**

WRITER DIRECTOR'S NOTE

One of the most interesting things about writing the *Millers Point Songbook* is that I didn't grow up with this history. It was all new to me, so I was coming at this with great curiosity and no 'cultural cringe.' Millers Point is a new name, coined during the early Colonial period and I have tried to acknowledge that by writing the opening song, 'Every Sunbed hides a Ghost.' When I arrived in this country I was shocked to see how little Aboriginal history was reflected in public places. That is changing somewhat now, and, while those are not my stories to tell, 'Every Sunbed' is a way of acknowledging the lost First Nations souls of the area before it was 'named.' In many of the history books I read, information about women and their roles in the neighbourhood was scant or simply absent. I have tried to address by writing as many songs as possible from a female perspective.

In terms of the musical vision, I see the piece as 'Folk Cabaret.' I began by listening to sea shanties, Irish and Scottish jigs, and traditional English ballads. I let these percolate, then married them with strong local characters telling a story, with simple repeated choruses. The idea is to create a convivial neighbourhood pub culture where people clap along and sing communally.

From the directing point of view, it is a great honour to have been given the opportunity to work in a site-specific way, rehearsing and performing the show in the beautiful Garrison Church, while reflecting on the time in which it was built. I have directed the marvellous community choir, Choir Rocks, for 12 years now and, while singers come and go, there is a core group who have now grown into a company.

I am so proud of the way they have embraced this project and brought their energies and talents along, from creating props and sourcing costumes, to donating their time to fundraising performances. The principal cast and musicians are outstanding professionals with whom I have worked before in various productions and I can't wait to hear how the music sounds in their care. Lastly, to you the audience, both local and from farther afield, you are invited to approach the show as yours, to clap along and join in where invited. Together we will bring this work to life.

—Joanna Weinberg

Choir Rocks: *front row: Jennifer Keeler-Milne, Joanna Weinberg, Annerose de Jong, Margaret Bishop, Michelle McDonald. second row: Dot Kolentsis, Chris Murphy. third row: Francisca van Wel, Sue Hunt, Cormac Chapion, James Hart. fourth row: Chris Russell, Craig Keeler-Milne, Michael Russell, Harley Nash.* **photo by Geoff Sirmai**

over page:
Rocks laneway (Downshire Street, Dawes Point), c.1935, **photo by Charles Walton**, SLNSW

THE LYRICS

HOTEL

EVERY SUNBED HIDES A GHOST

All across fair Sydney's coast,
Every sunbed hides a ghost.
Tanning flesh beyond the pale,
Sunshine lights a murky tale.
This same water lapped at feet which
Years ago cruel fate did meet.

Sydney's feet now swim and play and
Shadowed caverns silent stay.
Kicking backwards all through time,
Swimmers can't avoid the crime,
Wrought upon souls innocent,
By Empire with her vile intent.

Here upon this sunlit strand,
Children laughed upon the sand.
Fathers stood here with a spear,
Women fished in waters clear,
One thing that we know for sure,
It's not like that any more.

NAMING MILLERS POINT, 1833

Jack the Miller had 3 wooden mills,
3 wooden mills, 3 wooden mills.
Jack the Miller had 3 wooden mills
and he came a-tumbling down.

In 1833, the Millers Point economy,
Had captains of the industry,
Setting their sails for sea.

The soldiers are drinking,
  the convicts are rowing,
The governor's thinking,
  the colony's growing.
The publican's smuggling,
  the children are betting,
The mothers are struggling
  and everyone's sweating
In Millers Point.

In 1833, the Millers Point economy,
Had captains of the industry,
Setting their sails for sea.

The cartwheels are turning,
  the axes are cutting,
The middens are burning,
  the fishers are gutting,
The empire is stealing,
  the locals are looting,
The lashes are healing,
  the soldiers are shooting,
In Millers Point.

Windmills turning, home fires burning.
Land is clearing, ties are tearing.
Letters writing, factions fighting.

Jack the Miller had 3 wooden mills,
3 wooden mills, 3 wooden mills.
Jack the Miller had 3 wooden mills
and he came a-tumbling down.
In Millers Point.

Don't climb a ladder when you've
  drunk your fill,
Drunk your fill, drunk your fill.
Don't climb a ladder when you've
  drunk your fill,
Or you'll come a-tumbling down.

CAPTAIN GRIMES' RECRUITING SONG

Is your landlubber life dry and dull?
Do you want to feel awake?
Do you ever dream of a manful team
And of riches you could make?

Do you crave adventure, travel, fun?
Vivid stories you could share?
Well sit right down and have some grog,
And my motive I'll declare.

I am the trusty Captain Grimes
I sail the fair *Woodlark*.
On whaling expeditions she's
A most dependent barque.

For Lamps and lanterns light our way
Our Millers Point is dark,
And Oil we need for candles,
So soon we must embark.

I need some twenty sailors
With muscle and with will.
I need some twenty whalers
With power and with skill.

To wield the mighty blubber hooks
The lances and harpoon,
To hunt the beast with silver flesh
Beneath the Southern Moon.

Our women need their corsets tight,
All made from whale baleen.
And soap from whales is what they need
To keep their children clean.

The oil she gives is what we need
To keep the lighthouse bright,
Without it keels and mizzenmasts
Go missing in the night.

I need some twenty sailors
With muscle and with will.
I need some twenty whalers
With power and with skill.

To wield the mighty blubber hooks
The lances and harpoon.
To hunt the beast with silver flesh
Beneath the Southern Moon.

The ocean's full of danger
Haphazard and remote.
And anything could happen
Upon our whaling boat.

So I have for you a contract
It's sound and water tight.
I'll pay you decent wages,
If you sign for it tonight.

I need some twenty sailors
With muscle and with will.
I need some twenty whalers
With power and with skill.

To wield the mighty blubber hooks,
The lances and harpoon.
To hunt the beast with silver flesh
Beneath the Southern Moon.

Tomorrow you'll be sailing,
Away from Sydney shore.
This lushy joint in Millers Point,
Will be your home no more.

For as you glug your moonshine,
Your reason slowly wanes.
My first mate he is lurking,
To clap you into chains.

I need some twenty rough scum
To do my dirty work
I need some twenty tough scum
To suffer in the murk.

To man the stinking furnace
To hack with rusty knives
To hoist my sails and kill my whales
And promise me their lives.

MARY UNDERWOOD, WIFE OF THE CAPTAIN

My name was Mary Underwood,
I used to be a beauty.
But time has passed and now my mast
Is bending from her duty.

I know my Captain Grimes is brave
And storms at sea are Shocking.
But sad to say I run away
Each time his ship is Docking.

I am the wife of the Captain
I'm also the mother of ten
I say to you fine ladies,
Avoid seafaring men.
They get so miserable out at sea
A plateful of tarts they'd like for tea
And no that isn't enough for me
I'm living the life
Of trouble and strife
The lonely wife of a whaler.

My husband's name is Captain Grimes
He's out at sea a whaling.
While I am stuck [it's just my luck]
On shore with ten kids wailing.

He comes to us but once a year
With coconuts and pheasant,
He has his fun and when he's done
He leaves me with a present]

I am the wife of the Captain
I'm also the mother of ten
I say to you fine ladies,
Avoid seafaring men.
They get so miserable out at sea
A plateful of tarts they'd like for tea
And no that isn't enough for me
I'm living the life
Of trouble and strife
The lonely wife of a whaler.

I know we need the whaling oil
To keep our lamps a-burning.
But his harpoon returns in June
And I for rest am yearning.

My hands are cracked my nails are torn
For ten kids I am washing,
He thinks it's love but stars above
His lance I feel like squashing.

I am the wife of the Captain
I'm also the mother of ten
I say to you fine ladies,
Avoid seafaring men.
They get so miserable out at sea
A plateful of tarts they'd like for tea
And no that isn't enough for me
I'm living the life
Of trouble and strife
The lonely wife of a whaler.

I'LL NOT TAKE PART (DAWES, 1791)

You taught me as you fought with me
With eyes of rain and thunder.
We taught to you a lesson back
Of gunpowder and plunder.

My mind you have awoken,
But we have left you broken.
To me your country's thrilling
I'll not take part in killing.

Your fishing lines from *kurrajong*
The stories of your skies.
The wonder of your *wobbegong*
Our land clearing and lies.

Our stealing and our sailing
Has left your people ailing.
To me your country's thrilling
I'll not take part in killing.

Your *waradah* and your *warragul*
The fierceness of your sun.
Your *wumara*, your *goowawi*
Met powder from our gun.

To me you were forgiving
But we destroyed your living.
To me your country's thrilling
I'll not take part in killing.

WASHER WOMEN 1820

We're the women who take in the washing.
The women a washing your shirt.
The women who take in the washing,
Are the women who know all your dirt.

The smell of grog is awful,
The smell of shit is worse.
The smell of upchuck pudding
Will put me in a hearse.

The washing of the gentry,
All petticoats and lace,
While papa's at the whorehouse,
With knickers on his face.

We're the women who take in the washing.
The women a washing your shirt
The women who take in the washing,
Are the women who know all your dirt.

The soldier wears white linen,
The settler peed his sheets.
This governmental uniform,
Is full of fecking pleats.

This one's got her monthlies,
And this one's likely dead.
I think I'd rather sail away
On whaling boats instead.

We're the women who take in the washing.
The women a washing your shirt
The women who take in the washing,
Are the women who know all your dirt.

We tiptoe round the puddles,
Avoiding all the rats.
But don't you think we're free for tea
For now we wash our brats.

We long to putt our feet up,
A life with no more pain.
But dirt will wait for no-one.
Look, here it comes again.

We're the women who take in the washing.
The women a washing your shirt
The women who take in the washing,
Are the women who know all your dirt.

THE MURDER BALLAD OF ANNE KIRKMAN

Down in the Hero of Waterloo
A tune will set it's hooks in you,
It chills your blood as it passes through
For no-one is playing the piano.

What did I do to earn my fate?
Did I anger my man? Cause his hate?
No all I did was forget his plate
So carried away by my tune.

In eighteen-hundred-and-forty-nine
I sang my tune for the final time
My piano keys were my only friend,
And they played while I met my end.

I promised a fresh and tasty pie
'With ale to wash it down' said I
But by and by the time did fly
And no dinner did I supply.

I heard his lusty voice bellow
'Woman oh woman I hunger so'
Up the stairs from the bar below
His footsteps came a tramping.

In eighteen-hundred-and-forty-nine
I sang my tune for the final time
My piano keys were my only friend,
And they played while I met my end.

'I know' I cried 'I've done you wrong'
I did not mean to play so long.
My heart was lost within my song
I made a fatal blunder.

I smelled the ale, the floor, the chairs
As blood it flowed in crimson flares
My husband threw me down the stairs
For being too forgetful.

In eighteen-hundred-and-forty-nine
I sang my tune for the final time
My piano keys were my only friend,
And they played while I met my end.

The moral of my sorry tale,
Keep your promise without fail,
And stay away from a drunken male,
With dinner expectations.

THE AUSTRALIAN MERINO

We started out as Spanish mate,
Baaat that didn't last long,
We bred with Brits and Yankees,
And now our wool is strong.

They load our wool in Millers Point,
And squish it up in baaaaales.
We dominate the industry
Lucky for the whaaaales.

Australian Merino
We say this most Emphatic,
Our wool it warms the whole world up
What's more it's anti-static.

Myself I aaaam a champion
My Pedigree pure chaaarm.
I was bred by Elizabeth
Upon Macarthur's Faaaaarm.

We're bloody international now
Our wool is made to laaast.
5 warehouses on Windmill Street
We fill them up mate, faaaast,

Australian Merino
We say this most Emphatic
Our wool it warms the whole world up
What's more it's anti-static.

Last year I made a blanket,
Although my shearing hurt.
This year I made a caaaarpet
And next I'll make a skirt.

I like to make a uniform
Complete with wool felt hat.
I like to keep a soldier warm
Baa baa I'll drink to that.

Australian Merino
We say this most Emphatic
Our wool it warms the whole world up
What's more it's anti- static.

Queen Vic has worn my wool you know,
A lovely little shaaawl.
I heard she wore it in her bed,
And even to a baaaall.

Our wool is bloody famous mate
Though a relative newcomer.
We keep you warm in winter and
We keep you cool in summer.

Australian Merino
We say this most Emphatic
Our wool it warms the whole world up
What's more it's anti-static.

I had a little ewe last month
Her baaaa and horns were sweet.
But our affair was so short lived
They took her for her meat.

We're really quite maaaaagnificent
In Spring a fine aesthetic
But once they've sheared us to the bone
We look a bit pathetic.

Australian Merino
We say this most Emphatic
Our wool it warms the whole world up
What's more it's anti-static.

TED BRADY ON A SOAPBOX DURING THE MARITIME STRIKE OF 1890

Fair ladies and fine gentlemen,
A minute of your time.
For while you stroll the green Domain,
Nearby unfolds a crime.

I tell you of injustice grave,
It won't be to your liking.
For down upon the Millers Point,
The wharfies are a-striking.

They threw me out and fired me
Those money hungry sharks
I would not crack the crowns of mates
I've read the work of Marx.

A shilling was their payment
For a day of grinding length.
And who will help improve their lot?
They need a union's strength.

Sometimes the work it does not come
How grievous is their need.
Some 700 on the wharf,
Desperate for a feed.

They threw me out and fired me
Those money hungry sharks
I would not crack the crowns of mates
I've read the work of Marx.

The system of the wharf is false,
With bribes paid to the firm.
Whoever's in a gang gets work
The leftovers can squirm.
The shearers they are unionised
And wharfies help their mates.
But now we are the marked men
With nothing on our plates.

They threw me out and fired me
Those money hungry sharks
I would not crack the crowns of mates
I've read the work of Marx.

For true men now are demonised,
By class and by the press.
Dubbed 'thugs and crimps and larrikins,'
In truth they just have less.

They smashed up our rebellion
Our pride was badly torn
But from these grave injustices
A party will be born.

They threw me out and fired me
Those money hungry sharks
I would not crack the crowns of mates
I've read the work of Marx.

I know the pull of hunger.
No longer am I fat
The poet of the working man,
The proletariat.

You stand there in your finery,
'A madman' you decry.
But when you're finished judging me
Could you shout me a pie?

They threw me out and fired me
Those money hungry sharks
I would not crack the crowns of mates
I've read the work of Marx.

I liked my time at Millers Point
But for the South I'm bound.
I'm heading down to Melbourne now.
I'll see you all around.

THE SHANTY OF DRUNK NURSEY

I am drunk Nursey with Seamen I'm able,
Because I can drink them right under the table.

She is drunk Nursey with Seamen she's able,
Because she can drink them right under the table.

La di da la di all day.

I am drunk Nursey I'm no longer nursing,
I've packed it all in for carousing and cursing.

She is Drunk Nursey she's no longer nursing,
She's packed it all in for carousing and cursing.

La di da la di all day.

I am Drunk Nursey my fists make men nervous,
But me and my women give soldiers good service.

She is Drunk Nursey her fists make men nervous,
But she and her women give soldiers good service.

La di da la di all day.

I am Drunk Nursey I box with the sailors,
And when they are flattened I sing with the whalers.
She is Drunk Nursey she boxes with sailors
And when they are flattened I sing with the whalers.

La di da la di all day.

I am drunk Nursey I'm loving and giving,
And there's nothing wrong with how I make my living!

THE SONG OF MAYBANKE ANDERSON AND HER FOLLOWERS

I'm Maybanke, I'm a writer and I'm proudly middle class.
To women and their children I see troubles come to pass.
My paper is the Women's Voice *where new ideas I float,*
And so I will continue on until we have the vote.

My husband up and left me, yet I had no recourse.
I tried for several weary years, to legally divorce.
My husband owned my property, I could not make a will,
So I turned to public speaking and said, 'Let's reform the Bill.'

It seems to me that New South Wales has fundamental flaws,
As women don't participate in making of the laws.
And so to grow young women's minds I've given them a tool,
And opened up a forward thinking radical new school.

I'm Maybanke, I'm a writer and I'm proudly middle class.
To women and their children I see troubles come to pass.
My paper is the Women's Voice *where new ideas I float,*
And so I will continue on until we have the vote.

The Kindergarten Union has called on me to lead.
The infants of Australia are in dramatic need.
The leaders of the future, they need somewhere to be,
And every kindergarten must remain completely free.

The children here in Millers Point are roaming dirty streets.
They're ragged and uncared for and they beg the rich for treats.
I'm starting up a school for free where little ones can learn,
And mothers can go out to work their living for to earn.

I'm Maybanke, I'm a writer and I'm proudly middle class.
To women and their children I see troubles come to pass.
My paper is the Women's Voice *where new ideas I float,*
And so I will continue on until we have the vote.

It's poverty that puts women and girls onto the street,
And nobody yet faults the married men they go to meet.
A fourteen-year-old maiden for such treatment was not meant,
So we meet to try raise up the age of her consent.

Our meetings are held at the tea room of Quong Tart,
'Equality is equity' is how we always start.
The item for today is how to ban 'conjugal rights,'
And help the hapless married wife to sleep safely at nights.

I'm Maybanke, I'm a writer and I'm proudly middle class.
To women and their children I see troubles come to pass.
My paper is the Women's Voice *where new ideas I float,*
And so I will continue on until we have the vote.

So on I go to fight my fight and say what I must say.
And make playgrounds for children so that they can safely play.
I've worked for women all my life and done the best I can,
And now I've scandalised the town, with a younger man.

One day when we have won the vote don't think that I will cease.
I'll fight for children's schooling, and female expertise.
An educated woman can always set the pace,
And make sure that she leaves the world a slightly better place.

THE RATS OF MILLERS POINT

We're travellers we see the world,
We love the sound of sails unfurled.
When journey's done we case the street,
There ain't much that rats don't eat.

We came here as stowaways,
On Settler ships in early days,
Heard the talk, of the hour,
Millers point would have good flour.

We leave sinking ships for dead,
We like floating ones instead.
We climb ship ropes with our claws
And once in port we hit the shores.

Parasites to us endemic,
We're the bringers of pandemic.
We get infected by sick fleas,
We don't start the damn disease.

Millers Point was hot and damp,
Pretty soon the plague was ramp.
We just get it, then we spread it,
We're unpopular, you said it.

We leave sinking ships for dead,
We like floating ones instead.
We climb ship ropes with our claws
And once in port we hit the shores.

Arthur Paine of Ferry Lane,
He caught the plague, but then again,
Thomas Dudley popped a boil,
Shuffled off this mortal coil.

Round about us rattys ran,
While Sydneysiders kicked the can,
Ratcatchers came with disgust,
To make us rodents bite the dust.

We leave sinking ships for dead,
We like floating ones instead.
We climb ship ropes with our claws
And once in port we hit the shores.

Millers Point got scoured clean,
Poor folks stuck in quarantine.
Friends of ours incinerated,
Thought we'd be obliterated.

44 thousand hearts,
Stopped their beating round these parts.
Humans got off nearly free,
Total death count 103.

We leave sinking ships for dead,
We like floating ones instead.
We climb ship ropes with our claws
And once in port we hit the shores.

Enter the local government
Who redeveloped with cement
The wharves and seawalls there today
But *Rattus Rattus* is here to stay.

Even now in modern times,
We find haven in your climes.
Take your car, while you park it
We'll be at the farmers market.

We leave sinking ships for dead,
We like floating ones instead.
We climb ship ropes with our claws
And once in port we hit the stores.

THE RESUMPTION OF MILLERS POINT

'The Government of New South Wales,
Is buying up this joint,
One million pounds will buy for them,
The Rocks and Millers Point. '
[They say it's all about the plague,
That makes *me* want to laugh,]
Yeah, it's written here in black and white in
The *Daily Telegraph*.

'The dark and dirty alleys
Are full of grime and stink.
Wild larrikins and evil men
Might push you in the drink.
The foreigners and sailors,
Bring crowding and disease.'
The gambling dens and brothels
Bring the Irish and the fleas.

Clean it up! Clean it up! Clean it up!
Bring a hammer, knock it down.
Clean it up! Clean it up! Clean it up!
For Modern Sydney Town.

'The rich are running fastest,
Off to the other side.
They say our muck and grimy ways
Will spoil their civic pride.'
There's summing ere that don't feel right,
They'll squeeze out all our juice.
There's something that they wants from us,
Resumption means excuse.

'The madams and the prostitutes
Pick this place to hide.
And this is where the plague began.'
[Although only 3 died.]
'You'll see dead pets and excrement
The smells are not too nice.
It isn't classed as human,
On the shores of Paradise.'

Clean it up! Clean it up! Clean it up!
Bring a hammer, knock it down.
Clean it up! Clean it up! Clean it up!
For Modern Sydney Town.

I was born at Millers Point,
My house is spick and span.
My mother and grandmother too,
But that don't suit their plan.
I tell you what they're up to
Those toffs atop the ridge.
They're going to knock our houses down
To make a harbour bridge!

PERSPECTIVE

Our history lies not within your rusty book,
But in eyes of ancients which take the long look,
All stories will change with the teller of tales,
There's one for the hammer and one for the nails.

The land of my mother's will never be mine,
Until night is day and the sun doesn't shine,
The ground that I walk on is owned by the sky,
But no-one will notice till pigs start to fly.

The clocks don't keep time and the seasons don't tick,
The doctors don't know why the people fall sick.
The waves from the heavens look tiny and white,
The waves when you're drowning look black as the night.

Our history lies not within your rusty book,
But in eyes of ancients which take the long look,
All stories will change with the teller of tales,
There's one for the hammer and one for the nails.

THE SYDNEY HARBOUR TRUST

We'll shake your hand and take your land,
We'll modernise, and we'll expand,
We'll fill the air with noise and dust,
We are the Sydney Harbour Trust.

This rotten house has been condemned.
The tide of rodents has been stemmed.
We'll raze it all and build a wall,
For bigger ships bring work to all.

For Millers Point the past is fraught,
Our vision is a modern port,
We'll chop this tree, build shops for free,
Why look, here's electricity!

We'll shake your hand and take your land,
We'll modernise, and we'll expand,
We'll fill the air with noise and dust,
We are the Sydney Harbour Trust.

You live right here upon the shore,
Admit it's better than before,
We'll build you flats, and you'll work for us,
Here comes a shiny omnibus.

Our policies will bring great joy
To every man and every boy,
You residents have got it made,
Behold the Hotel Palisade.

We'll shake your hand and take your land.
We'll modernise, and we'll expand,
We'll fill the air with noise and dust,
We are the Sydney Harbour Trust.

We wear our ties, you wear your boots,
We give you houses where it suits.
You'll find it new, you'll find it strange,
But we bring vital urban change.

The die is cast, It's happening fast,
Your recent past it cannot last.
Forget the filth of recent years,
Embrace our sparkling shiny piers.

We'll shake your hand and take your land,
We'll modernise, and we'll expand,
We'll fill the air with noise and dust,
We are the Sydney Harbour Trust.

DOWN WITH DRINK, 1916

We're fighting for The Empire,
To save our promised land,
And our young men are training,
To leave and lend a hand.

But alcohol has weakened
The morals of our sons,
And so we call to ban it all,
From soldiers with their guns.

Down with Drink, the soldiers are fighting in the streets of Sydney,
Down with Drink, they're looting the shops and throwing bricks.
Down with Drink, the gutters are running full of piss and whisky,
Down with Drink, we call for the pubs to close at six.

Our Union loves Temperance,
Of Christian Women made.
There's drinking all around us,
And nightly we're afraid.

A man who's full of liquor,
His eye with madness twists.
He beats at any in his path
With mighty drunken fists.

Down with Drink, the soldiers are fighting in the streets of Sydney,
Down with Drink, they're looting the shops and throwing bricks.
Down with Drink, the gutters are running full of piss and whisky,
Down with Drink, we call for the pubs to close at six.

A woman full of liquor,
Too soon will feel the cost,
Her pearls she'll cast before a swine,
And then her virtue's lost.

And when with liquor mates she makes
Her nightly life runs wild,
Why see out on the step there sits
Another lonely child.

Down with Drink, the soldiers are fighting in the streets of Sydney,
Down with Drink, they're looting the shops and throwing bricks.
Down with Drink, the gutters are running full of piss and whisky,
Down with Drink, we call for the pubs to close at six.

Outside every pub there waits
A ragged little waif.
O Women we must play our role,
To keep our children safe.

Come join us suffering sisters
Come take an angry hand.
Come find your strength along the length
Of our determined band.

Down with Drink, the soldiers are fighting in the streets of Sydney,
Down with Drink, they're looting the shops and throwing bricks.
Down with Drink, the gutters are running full of piss and whisky,
Down with Drink, we call for the pubs to close at six.

THE FATEFUL JOURNEY OF THE SS *CERAMIC*, 29 APRIL 1942

Sail sweet *Ceramic*, keep my lover safe.
Bring home a paycheck or two,
Buy me a lipstick in Liverpool, Love.
Make sure to Sydney you're true.

Keep up your smiling sweet love of my life
As you sail off for the war.
I will be waiting, Dear, for your return,
Here on the Millers Point shore.

Wave me goodbye as you leave for the sea.
I'll toss my hat in the crowd,
You will not get a white feather from me.
I will be lonely but proud.

Keep up your smiling sweet love of my life
As you sail off for the war.
I will be waiting, Dear, for your return,
Here on the Millers Point shore.

In the Atlantic, so cold and so grey,
Slowly you sank to the floor.
Harry and Bertie my brother, and James,
Sacrificed all for the war.

Keep up your smiling sweet love of my life
As you sail off for the war.
I will be waiting, Dear, for your return,
Here on the Millers Point shore.

STREET SONG

music and lyrics by Sue Hunt

My dear how are you, are you battling through?
I baked this morning there's a cake for you.
That will be lovely you are very kind.
You're looking out for me so I'll be fine.

And how's that leg of yours are you in pain?
Fair to middling thanks I can't complain.
The doctor looks in every day at nine.
She's looking out for me so I'll be fine.

But who's the fellow in the Paddock there?
Sleeping rough out in the chilly air?
I give him breakfast I don't know his name.
We all look out for him just the same.
Just the same. Just the same.
We all look out for him just the same.
Just the same.

UPSTAIRS IN THE FRONT ROOM, 1945

Babies are born ba-ba ba,
Babies are born ba-ba ba,
Babies are being born.

No-one calls the doctor,
They call on us instead.
We call all the women
To help at Mother's bed.

Mrs Flynn's is popping,
We think today's the day.
We've delivered seven, now eight is on its way, Hey, hey, hey hey, hey.

Rock a baby, little baby
Soon it's time to see the world.
Rock a baby little baby maybe you will be a girl.

We are the midwives, of Millers Point
We're sensible and down to earth,
We're the midwives, of Millers Point
And we help you to give birth.

Upstairs in the front room,
Is where all babes are born.
No-one goes to hospital
Unless something goes wrong.

Some young women,
Can't attend the show,
We can help them manage,
And nobody will ever know,
Oh, oh, oh, oh, oh, oh.

Rock a baby, little baby soon it's time for mother's joy.
Rock a baby little baby maybe this one is a boy.

Because we're the midwives,
of Millers Point
Sensible, and down to earth,
We're the midwives, of Millers Point
And we help you to give birth.

THE CONTAINER KING

I was just a simple trucker,
Driving goods to earn my tucker.
Went down to the wharf for chips yeah,
Watched them loading up the ships there.
Took the men a week to offload.
What if trucks were not just onroad?
That's how I had my great notion
Transport boxes on the ocean.
Could I be the new trend-setter ?
Giant boxes even better.
Lock the boxes with tight chains,
No more quick ill-gotten gains.

Talking containerisation.
Talking containerisation.
I started globalisation.
He started globalisation.

Here's a little fact explainer,
You can stack a flat container.
Bought an old tanker to try it,
Stacked more goods and caused a riot.
Saw the future they weren't seeing,
Let's use cranes not human beings.

Ships of guns or gold or gravel,
All around the globe they travel.
Consumers give me their devotion,
I move their stuff across the ocean.
I was a dumb-ass kid in torn up britches,
Now I'm rolling deep in riches.

Talking containerisation.
Talking containerisation.
I started globalisation.
He started globalisation.

NITA McCRAE PETITIONS TO SAVE THE ROCKS FROM HIGHRISE DEVELOPMENT, 1970

I'm just ordinary,
Nothing much to see.
But like a rolling bottle,
I don't stop easily.
When I get to rolling,
Best get out the way.
Nothing's made of tougher stuff than me
Nita McCrae.

Got no fancy label,
Got no necklace long.
Got a bloody brilliant sense,
Of when you do me wrong.
Every time you throw me,
Trying to break my back,
I will come back stronger,
For every little crack.

I'm writing letters,
Every single day.
I'm writing letters,
Getting in the way.
You're not my betters,
You don't have the say.
Because I'll write another letter every day,
Until I find someone to join the fray,
To save the place my friends and
neighbours stay.

JACK MUNDEY'S GREEN BAN, 1973

Why, why would you break this town?
Flatten our history down?
You got it all so wrong.
Who are you hiding from?
You think that you're so tough.
You can't scrub hard enough
To put on a human face.
Leave us a friendly place.

See all of the workers rise,
Under the Sydney skies,
Standing on moral ground,
History comes around.

What are you scared of city bright?
That they won't think you've got it right.
Just because it is big and white,
Don't make it beautiful.
You're so ashamed my Sydney Sweet.
All of the past beneath your feet.
Nothing wrong with an old-time street,
In fact, it's beautiful.

So when they come to hire us
We will say No! We will say No!
Threaten us, and fire us,
We will say No! We will say No!
When they want destruction
We will say No! We will say No!
When they want construction
We will say No! We will say No!

THE SALE OF SIRIUS TO DEVELOPERS

Welcome to the listing of the year!
Brutalist, it's iconic.
Stunning, it is Sydney reinvented!
Where millionaires can frolic.
Welcome to historic reinvention,
That somehow looks brand new.
This gem started life as social housing.
But they had a killer
But they had a killer
But they had a killer view.

More than the story of a building,
This is the story of our home.
One day we tenants got a letter
Which turned our hearts right into stone.
Government wanted relocation.
Community was getting old.
Seemed we were all facing eviction,
For the greater good
For the greater good
For the greater good we're told.

That's life. Nothing lasts forever.
It was good for a while.
Sydney is a thriving global city
With international style.
They found every one of you a new home.
They helped you relocate.

New friends, living in new places
Not a miserable
Not a miserable
Not a miserable fate.

Our small community was thriving,
Felt just like a country town.
We only ever knew this city,
We did not bring our Sydney down.
We felt connected to our history.
Cos we could walk down to the Quay.
Sold for a 150 million,
Property is not
Property is not
Property is not for me.

Richard Briggs, *Save Our Souls*, pen on paper, 2017

Sirius, Sirius, Sirius,
Where we could leave our cares.
Sirius Sirius Sirius
A home for millionaires.
Sirius Sirius Sirius
Which had a higher goal.
Sirius Sirius Sirius
Now who will save your soul?

Sirius, where we could leave our cares.
Sirius, a home for millionaires.
Sirius, which had a higher goal.
Sirius, now who will save your soul?

FINALE: THE SPIRIT OF MILLERS POINT
music and lyrics by Sue Hunt

You'll see me early evening at the Hero,
The light falls gently now on those sandstone tales of old.
Voices past a soft and distant echo.
Walls that whisper the wisdom that they hold.

Friday lunch it's a beer at the Lord Nelson,
Neighbours night at the Captain Cook Hotel.
It's the Palisades or the Harbour View for parties.
You get all the news from neighbours there as well.
There are unsung heroes living all around us.
All working hard towards a future bright and bold.
Raise a glass as you listen to their stories.
You know history continues to unfold.
Celebrate as the morning stars among us
Shine the way and illuminate the dawn.
They are championing ten thousand new beginnings.
As the spirit of Millers Point lives on.

FINALE: PAVE THE WAY, MEL'S SONG
music and lyrics by Sue Hunt

Millers Point in someways is like every other place,
Addicted to buying brand new things that all end up in waste.
If the unused council shed across the street could see rebirth,
Could we cut down local wastage and champion the earth?

If we pave the way,
Habits change,
Step by step,
Steady gains.
If we pave the way,
Habits change,
Step by step,
Steady gains.

So I turned the empty shed into a new recycling hub.
The locals drop their old things off on their way to the pub.
Old toys and books and boxes, batteries, bags of clothes.
Reducing landfill isn't hard, with a pub just down the road.

If we pave the way.
Habits change,
Step by step,
Steady gains.
If we pave the way,
Habits change,
Step by step,
Steady gains.

Millers Point in history has seen recklessness and greed.
So quick to cast aside what doesn't service the current need.
Can we champion community that values all we share
Built on kindness and respect for everything that's rare?

If we pave the way,
Habits change,
Step by step,
Steady gains.
If we pave the way,
Habits change,
Step by step,
Steady gains.

FINALE: GEORGINA'S SONG
music and lyrics by Sue Hunt

Raised in a bustling family, all doctors down the line
It taught me to live life as if you're running out of time.
They say I'm the one who works hard, and plays hard every day.
A medical research career just seemed the obvious way.
Skin cancer kills Australians, almost forty every week,
For twenty years new treatments for melanoma did I seek.
This work is saving lives and so receiving world attention,
But the surest way to combat melanoma is prevention.

So...
Save your skin, that's all I ask.
Put skin cancer in the past.
Save your skin, that's all I ask.
Put skin cancer in the past.

The spotlight is so fleeting and already months have passed
But fear is not an option, no distraction from the task.
The say make use of this precious time is the obligation here
To pave the way for future work beyond this single year.
Can we harness immunology against many forms of cancer?
I'm championing research that could help provide the answer.
In Millers Point we've always put our mettle to the test.
My dream is zero deaths from melanoma, nothing less.

Let's...
Save our skin, that's the task
Put melanoma in the past.
Save our skin, that's the task
Put melanoma in the past.

FINALE: THE SPIRIT OF MILLERS POINT
music and lyrics by Sue Hunt

You'll see me early evening at the Hero,
The light falls gently now on those sandstone tales of old.
Voices past a soft and distant echo.
Walls that whisper the wisdom that they hold.

Friday lunch it's a beer at the Lord Nelson
Neighbours night at the Captain Cook Hotel.
It's the Palisades or the Harbour View for parties.
You get all the news from neighbours there as well.
There are unsung heroes living all around us.
All working hard towards a future bright and bold.
Raise a glass as you listen to their stories.
You know history continues to unfold.
Celebrate as the morning stars among us
Shine the way and illuminate the dawn.
They are championing ten thousand new beginnings.

As the spirit
As the spirit
As the spirit
As the spirit of Millers Point lives on.